Regarding the
Borgo Pio

Regarding the Borgo Pio

An Architectural View of a
Renaissance Street in Rome

Martha Sutherland

THE UNIVERSITY OF ARKANSAS PRESS

FAYETTEVILLE • 1996

00 99 98 97 96   5 4 3 2 1

Designed by Ellen Beeler

☉ The paper used in this publication meets the minimum
requirements of the American National Standard for Permanence
of Paper for Printed Library Materials Z39.48-1984.

Library of Congress Cataloging-in-Publication Data

Sutherland, Martha, [date]
     Regarding the Borgo Pio : an architectural view of a
renaissance street in rome / Martha Sutherland.
          p. cm.
     Includes bibliographical references.
     ISBN 1-55728-413-X (cloth : alk. paper). —ISBN 1-55728-
414-8 (paper : alk. paper)
     1. Via di Borgo Pio (Rome, Italy) 2. Streets—Italy—Rome.
3. Rome (Italy)—Buildings, structures, etc. 4. Architecture—
Italy—Rome. I. Title.
     DG815.9.V53S87   1996
     945'.632—dc20   95-38238
                                                   CIP

*This project was supported by a grant from the Graham Foundation for
Advanced Studies in the Fine Arts.*

Contents

*I*n the historic center of the city of Rome there are 1,989 streets and squares. A few of them boast a history of more than two thousand years. Many of them have been in place for five hundred years. The Via di Borgo Pio was born in the year 1562, so it is not the oldest street, nor is it the most beautiful or even the most notorious. But it has retained its character in a tenacious way, and the building spasms that remade a good part of Rome in the sixteenth century, in 1870, and again in 1937 skirted, but spared, Pius IV's street.

The Via di Borgo Pio came about, not by accident, or by "the force of inactivity," or by simple expansion. It was the result of two powerful dynamics—the ancient geography of the city and the rise of Christendom.

Rome proper, around the time of Christ, occupied the lowlands called the Campus Martius in the big bend of the Tiber, the seven hills and all the intervening areas, and the Trastevere across the river, up to the ridge of the Gianiculum Hill and down to the Mausoleum of Hadrian.

In addition to Hadrian's massive tomb, there were several important buildings in the Trastevere: a circus begun by Caligula and finished by Nero, a *naumachia* where water spectacles were held, and

a large funerary monument in the shape of a four-stepped marble pyramid, built for an unknown Roman family, although it later came to be called the Sepulcher of the Scipione. These structures were defining nodes for future urban development.

For the most part however, this area across the river was filled with gardens and summer houses belonging to the imperial family and to people of high rank. Behind a graceful portico at the river's edge, the Horti Agrippinae, or Gardens of Agrippina, sloped up the hill, suitably verdant and worthy of envy. With Agrippina's death in A.D. 33, they passed to her son Caligula and became a popular playground for the elite and for the degenerate later emperors, particularly Nero.

*O*ur story begins with the terrible fire of Rome in the year of our Lord 64. Reigning at the time was the infamous Nero, whose reputation was not helped at all by the widespread rumor that he set the fire himself in order to enjoy watching the city burn. To counteract the bad press, he offered space in Agrippina's

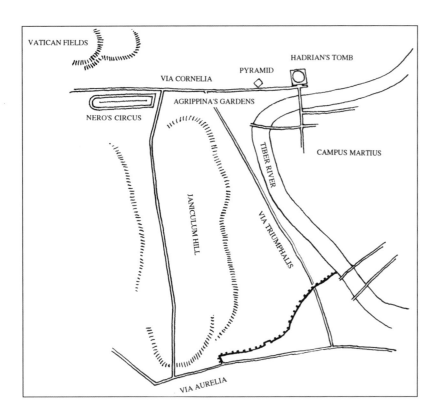

*Plan of Trastevere and the Vatican fields showing
the ancient roads and monuments.*

The map includes the following labels: VATICAN FIELDS, VIA CORNELIA, PYRAMID, HADRIAN'S TOMB, AGRIPPINA'S GARDENS, NERO'S CIRCUS, CAMPUS MARTIUS, TIBER RIVER, VIA TRIUMPHALIS, JANICULUM HILL, VIA AURELIA

gardens across the Tiber and below the Vatican Hill to survivors, even putting up temporary housing for them. When this failed to quell suspicions, he went on the offensive, claiming that it was the Christians who had started the fire and that they should be considered enemies of Rome. In a show of strength and barbarism, he set up an antique version of an auto-da-fé. Hundreds of Christians were slaughtered. According to Tacitus, many were crucified, many torn to pieces, and still others were spread with pitch and burned alive, becoming torches to light the gardens. Nasty voices said Nero had offered the gardens on purpose to provide himself yet another evening of sound and light. Reportedly the macabre tableau included the crucifixion of the apostle Peter.

The gardens were in an area known even then as the *ager vaticanus*, or vatican fields, giving its name later to the Vatican City. The gardens also housed the circus of crowd-pleasing scale begun by Caligula, important to us because the church of Saint Peter was constructed on part of its foundations. On the axis of the circus, Caligula had erected the giant obelisk stolen from Alexandria in Egypt. Today it stands in front of Saint Peter's Basilica.

Down by the waterside, around A.D. 130, the emperor Hadrian built his grandiose circular tomb and with it the bridge across the Tiber to allow access from the city. The tomb, now known as the Castel Sant' Angelo, was the last great pagan monument constructed in the Trastevere.

As the might of Rome weakened, it was inevitable that the ponderous mass of Hadrian's mausoleum would become part of a fortification system, particularly as its bridge afforded easy entry into the city of Rome to friend and foe alike. Some scholarship suggests that the emperor Aurelian in the third century incorporated the tomb into a defensive wall that took advantage of previous walls reaching from the crest of the Gianicolo to the river. The resulting roughly oval-shaped compound was called the *borgo*—a word probably descending from "burgus," a small fortified settlement.

The stage is now set for the second act of our drama. The Edict of Milan in 313 allowed citizens of the empire freedom of choice in their religion. The emperor Constantine, newly converted to Christianity and with the law on his side, built an important church on the ruins of the ancient circus near the spot where the apostle Peter had been martyred. Called Saint Peter's Church, it quickly became a magnet that attracted thousands of pilgrims to the little borough outside the city of Rome. The mystique of Saint Peter's Church soon eclipsed that of the cathedral of Saint John in Lateran across the river, which was by rights the home of the pope. In those days it was a long procession from the Lateran to the Vatican, often in the heat of the summer, so special apartments were soon built near the church to allow the pope to stay over. They became the nucleus of the Vatican Palace.

Constantine built the church, but then he moved the real seat of government to Constantinople, leaving a bureaucratic vacuum in Rome that the fledgling Catholic Church was only too happy to fill. One of its first tasks was to minister to and care for the waves of pilgrims eager to absorb sanctity at the tomb of Saint Peter.

As they are today, the crowds of tourists were a huge source of income and prestige. In the next several hundred years (from the fifth to the ninth century) innumerable hostels—embryonic hotels —were built, eventually stretching all the way from the church to the Castel Sant' Angelo inside the protective walls. These *scholae peregrinorum* were financed by the country of origin—Francia, Saxony, Frisia, Lombardia, and so on. Monasteries to house the clergy that manned the hostels became necessary. And there had to be hospitals because sickness and trauma were rife. Krautheimer cites one hospital that was exclusively for the footsore, a commentary on the great distances many pilgrims covered on foot. There was a poorhouse, many small churches, chapels, water fountains, and lavatories.

Among the hostels built by the motherlands of the pilgrims, England's has been particularly remembered through the centuries. In the eighth century, Ine, the king of Wessex, renounced his crown and came to Rome as a simple pilgrim. In the year 725 he founded the Schola Saxonum to care for his compatriots when they arrived to pray at the tomb of Saint Peter. It flourished for a time and was immortalized 476 years later in 1201 when Pope Innocent III established the Order of Santo Spirito on the Schola Saxonum site. This became the Ospedale di Santo Spirito in Sassia, or the Hospital of the Holy Spirit in Saxony, an organization still going strong today.

Of vital importance in protecting the growing settlement around Saint Peter's were the fortified walls of the borgo. They were continually maintained, modified, amplified, and strengthened until the 1600s. In the time of Charlemagne, Pope Leo III replaced the old system of walls with a stronger one that circled the emperor's palace, the schools, hospitals, and churches and attached itself, logically, to the impregnable bastions of the Castel Sant' Angelo. But when the pope died in 816, the Roman citizenry tore the new walls down to the ground because they feared the papacy was becoming too powerful—an act of supreme folly. In 846 the Saracens swept into the unprotected borgo like avenging angels, sacked the basilica, schools, and imperial palace, raped the women, burned, pillaged, and destroyed. As soon as the populace could work again, Leo IV had them rebuilding the defenses. The ancient pyramid, stripped of the slabs of marble to be used later in the steps of Saint Peter's, was incorporated into the new fortifications. The wall from the palace on the Vatican Hill down to the Castel Sant' Angelo was to become very important. One day in 1277, Pope Nicholas III was on the ramparts surveying his realm when he realized that the wall connecting his palace to his castle was potentially a *primo* escape route in case of danger. He acted on this idea, roofed most of the wall, and was proved right many times in the following centuries. The wall came to be known as the Corridori or the Passetto.

In the fourteenth century, the removal of the papacy to Avignon reduced the borgo to a calamitous state. It was the worst of depressions. The Hospital of Santo Spirito shut its doors, was abandoned, and fell into ruin. Rejuvenation came with the return of the popes in approximately 1350. In contrast to the rest of Europe, which was painfully suffering through arid economic times, the Catholic Church, holding the Tomb of Saint Peter to its bosom, was on the march toward a rich and splendid sixteenth century. On the upswing of this prosperity, Sixtus IV was able to afford a complete restoration of the Hospital of Santo Spirito.

The vast hospital complex was made up of a hostel for important visitors, a poorhouse, a maternity ward, a shelter for fallen women, and an orphanage and nursery for abandoned babies. Sadly, only fifty years after the restoration, the building was totally destroyed by the armies of Charles V. However, it was soon rebuilt along the same lines as before and is the building we see today, complete with historic memorabilia. The

ruota degli Esposti, or Wheel of the Exposed, is still in place on the side of the hospital building. It is a grated window screening a wooden door. Behind the door is a revolving platform on which a baby could be placed. The movement of the platform rang a bell which alerted those inside that the wheel was occupied. In this way, an unhappy mother could abandon a child but know that it would be taken care of.

During the black years while the popes cowered in Avignon, the walls of the borgo crumbled and cracked along with public morale, but after the triumphal return to Rome and about the same time that Columbus was discovering America, Alexander VI strengthened the fortifications yet again. He probably contracted with the famous architect Antonio da Sangallo il Vecchio for the job, and being pleased with the results, allowed him to design two battlemented towers for the Porta di San Pellegrino.

By the time the Hospital of Santo Spirito was restored in 1520, the borgo had been (as the Italians say) *systematized*. From the Castel Sant' Angelo, there were two roads leading north to Saint Peter's Basilica—the Via Alessandrina which became the Via di Borgo Nuovo, and the Via di

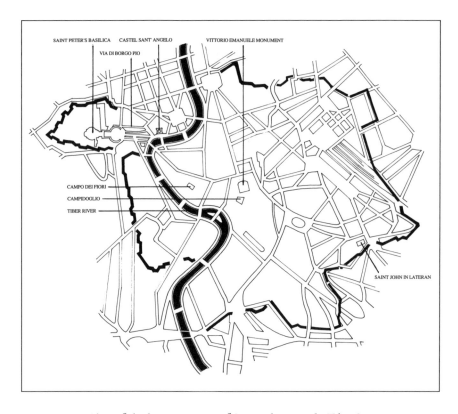

*Plan of the historic center of Rome, showing the Tiber River
and the ancient city walls.*

Borgo Vecchio which was probably the ancient Roman road. On the south there was the Via di Borgo Santo Spirito leading to the town gate, outside of which the ancient road traced the river south to the village of Trastevere. These refinements basically adjusted a perimeter that was in place in the year 1000 and retained it until 1938 when the Via della Conciliazione swept aside two of the old roads.

It was 1562. The Via di Borgo Pio was ready for its debut. Pius IV had just caused a new line of fortifications to be built. First he erected the pentagonal wall around the Castel Sant' Angelo that gives it its present distinctive outline, and from it he extended a new wall angling north of the Passetto and joined it to the farthest reach of the Vatican Palace bastion, below the Belvedere. The new wall rendered the Passetto unnecessary as a fortification. Pius promptly opened arches through its lower parts to allow passage into the newly created suburb— a very modern development. Seven passages were punched corresponding to seven cross streets,

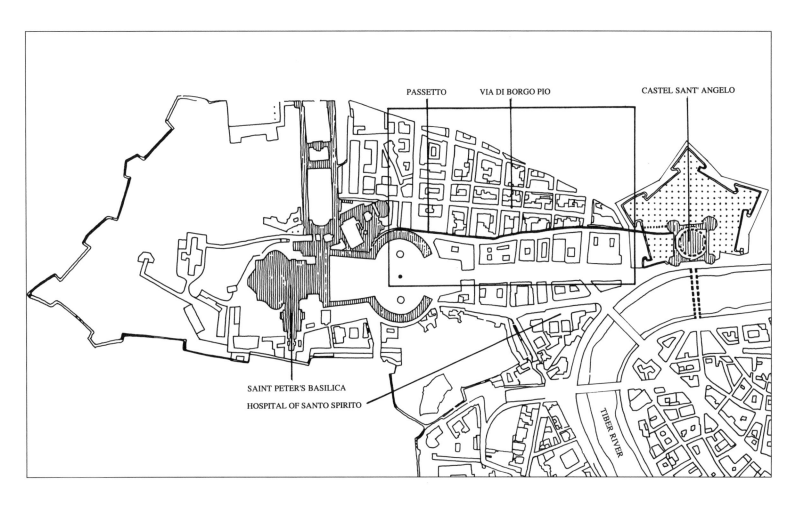

PASSETTO   VIA DI BORGO PIO   CASTEL SANT' ANGELO

SAINT PETER'S BASILICA

HOSPITAL OF SANTO SPIRITO

TIBER RIVER

Plan of the borgo showing Saint Peter's Basilica and the Castel Sant' Angelo.

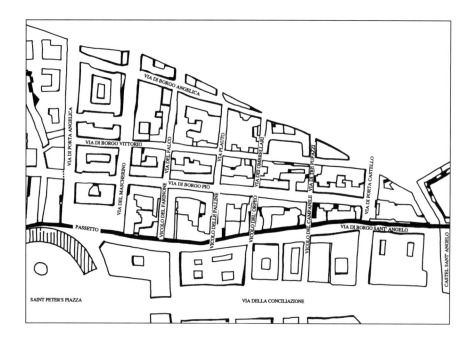

Detail of the Borgo Pio area.

making the gridded pattern so much at variance with any other part of old Rome. Leading north and south, the first street was the venerable Via di Porta Angelica closest to the Vatican Palace. Next, to the east comes the Via del Mascherino, then the Vicolo del Farinone, the Vicolo delle Palline, the Vicolo d' Orfeo, the Vicolo del Campanile, and finally the Via di Porta Castello. Parallel to the Via di Borgo Pio but on the other side of the Passetto, Pius IV opened the Via di Borgo Sant' Angelo by excising the hovels that stuck to the wall like barnacles. Pius IV's successor, Pius V, completed the grid by putting through one more east-west street, the Via Vittorio. All the buildings on the Via di Borgo Pio had their backs to the Passetto wall, inextricably linking the street and the wall as one unit. As the cross streets traversed Via di Borgo Pio several of them changed their names: Farinone to Via del Falco, Palline to Via Plauto, Orfeo to Via degli Ombrellari, and Campanile to Via dei Tre Pupazzi.

Although the Passetto was no longer a defensive wall, it did retain its function as an escape route. After Pope Nicholas III roofed it over, it became a secure egress from the Vatican Palace to the Gibraltar-like haven of the Castel.

8

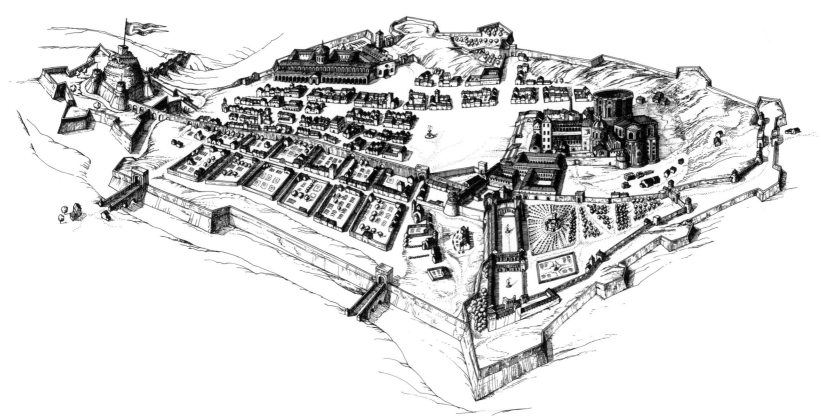

VIEW TO THE SOUTH c. 1578

THE BORGO OF ROME

M. SUTHERLAND

View of Saint Peter's from the Castel Sant' Angelo.

The corridor belonged exclusively to the pope, and only he had access to the keys. Alexander VI used them in 1494 to elude the clutches of Charles VIII of France. Pius III in 1503, to protect himself from the Orsini, hurried down the passage with his children, two pages, and four servants. Clement VII in 1526 fled into the fortress to escape the menace of the Moncadas and the Colonnas and repeated the journey several months later when the army of Emperor Charles V charged into Rome. From his impregnable rock castle, Clement witnessed a destruction so complete that it is a benchmark in the history of the city.

The wall today is a rich tapestry of colors and textures. Having undergone so many devastations, reconstructions, mendings, and patchings, it has no discernible style and no one primary building material. There are blocks of tufa and peperino, crumbling limestone, rows of brick, and modern cement. One can see arches that have been filled in and windows from all periods. Iron grills abound. Pigeons nest in the put holes; wildflowers grow in the cracks. The medieval crenelations march most of the way to the castle, creating an undulating crown topping the gentle curve of the route. There are large blotches of plaster, tinged here and there with color, that are traces of houses that were once built against the wall but torn down in the 1930s.

Naturally the popes who restored the wall left their imprimature as had the Roman emperors before them—a bit of propaganda for the masses. Pius IV ornamented every new street opening with the multi-pilled stemma of the Medici— it was these little balls that gave the Vicolo delle Palline its name. Alexander VI's striped insignia of the Borgia can still be seen, Clement VIII's raguly and Pius V's diagonal bars are there, and Pius IX's quartered arms proclaim his reconstruction of the arch that adjoined the Castel and that was demolished in 1849 by the Republican army.

A second arch was added to the ones at Via di Porta Angelica and Via del Mascherino in the 1930s and at the Via di Porta Castello in the 1950s to cope with the flood of automobile traffic. At the other end of the street, a second arch was added in 1937 for the same reason, and the stemma of Pius XI was affixed. Today one of the interesting proposals put before the Vatican by the city fathers is to shore up the Passetto and open it to tourists, thus perpetuating its useful life.

Arch of the Passetto at Vicolo d' Orfeo, showing the stemma of the Medici.

Papal stemmas on arches of the Passetto.

The development of the Via di Borgo Pio came at a time of transition in architectural style. The ascent of Pope Nicholas V in 1471 had cost the borgo much of its medieval look and introduced the glories of the Renaissance. Nicholas had not seen himself as the inventor of a new architectural idiom; indeed, his aim was more lofty. He envisioned buildings that could make church doctrine three dimensional. His dream was powerful enough to dictate the direction of religious architecture for several hundred years, and residually even into the twentieth century. In the words of Carroll Westfall, it even "unknowingly haunted Mussolini."

Nicholas built hoping that "his buildings would move men to love God." Architecture spoke to him in a way that painting and sculpture moved earlier popes. Nicholas's philosophy found a fellow spirit in the architect Leon Battista Alberti, one of the brilliant lights of the rebirth of classicism. It was to Nicholas that Alberti presented his book on architecture, *De Re Aedificatoria*. Nicholas, impressed, approached Alberti for advice on the enlargement and restructuring of the old church of Saint Peter on its mound above the sacred martyrium. Nicholas died before that project was born, but his vision for an urban plan clarifying the precincts of church and state outlived him.

As part of his great scheme, Nicholas did rebuild the Palazzo del Senatore on the Capitoline Hill, the better to create a dominant presence in the center of town that would emphasize the position of the body politic as separate from the body ecclesiastic across the river.

He had marginal faith in the Romans who ran the government, which in the quattrocento was nominally a republic. Allowing the laity a modicum of power softened the bald fact that it was the papacy that ruled. Nicholas's grand plan was meant to show that the church of Saint Peter dominated the city and that the borgo was separate from Rome. He strengthened the presence of the state on the one hand, while aggrandizing his own position by rebuilding Constantine's compound at the Vatican and moving in with all his retinue. After five hundred years the palace on the hill had won out over Saint John in Lateran.

When the Pope's residence became the Vatican, it seemed proper to raise the living

View of Vicolo d' Orfeo with the Passetto.

standards in the surrounding borgo. It was within the pontiff's power to offer wealthy parishioners exemptions from certain duties or even immunity from past crimes. Benefits like these were given in exchange for adding to the prestige of the area by building there in the grand manner. Naturally this approach achieved spectacular results. Cardinal Domenico della Rovere built his Renaissance palace on the Via di Borgo Vecchio. It is still there, called the Penitenzieri. Cardinal Alessandrino quickly followed suit. His palace is now the Collegio Santa Monica dei Patres Agostiniani. In 1496 it was Cardinal Adriano Castellesi's turn to build the beautiful Torlonia Palace, in place to this day.

The famous architects Bramante, Raphael, and Sangallo were among many who were happy to design *palazzos* for the new high-rent district. Their exciting new style gave the borgo a Renaissance flavor unique in Rome, which is essentially a baroque city.

Nicholas's ethic put down permanent roots. A few years later when Sixtus IV became pontiff, the new style was securely in place. Sixtus reconstructed the Hospital of Santo Spirito from its foundations up, à la the Renaissance. Part of the new look was the opening of the previously mentioned Via Alessandrina—one of the two streets leading from the Castel Sant' Angelo to Saint Peter's. It was opened in time for the Jubilee of 1500. The ancient pyramid was wiped out to put it through. Later the road was paved by Julius II in an overt display of self-interest. He was passionately fond of races and other contests and arranged for them to start at the Campo dei Fiori on the other side of the river and wanted them to end under his palace window at Saint Peter's Piazza without stirring up any mud or dust.

By the time Sixtus IV had embraced the Renaissance, Rome was already, and literally, on the map. Before this time, and throughout the Middle Ages, maps were odd collections of monuments and major buildings drawn in elevation or in distorted perspective and lumped together with practically no indication of streets or proper scale. The more important the building, the larger it was drawn. Gradually map making became more sophisticated.

The first extant map of Christian Rome was made in 1323 by Fra Paolino. It does little to further our knowledge of what was happening on the ground. By the time of the Schedel map of

1493 the region of the borgo with old Saint Peter's and the Vatican Palace was properly positioned, the Castel Sant' Angelo and the Passetto were marked, and the area beyond the Passetto depicted as the rolling farmland where most of the food for the city of Rome was grown. After Schedel, map making changed from an esoteric avocation to an established profession. In the biography of Rome, each new map, or plan, marked a chapter in the city's metamorphosis from the late medieval period until the present day.

In 1551 Leonardo Bufalini, a Renaissance topographer, issued a remarkable plan showing the streets and blocks clearly and precisely. Strangely enough, the building blocks and many monuments are shown in flat outline, and not drawn as three dimensional shapes as was done in almost all of the maps of the time. In fact, it is a modern map. The borgo is only a small section of the whole city, but the position of the Passetto, Saint Peter's, and the Castel Sant' Angelo are accurately delineated. The Via di Borgo Pio has not yet come into being.

Finally in 1576 is the plan by Mario Cartaro, showing the Via di Borgo Pio born at last and called by its Latin name—Via di Burgus Pius,

named in honor of Pope Pius IV who opened the new street. Pius's architect Francisco Laparelli contributed his expertise to the development. Already the seven blocks from the Vatican to the Castel Sant' Angelo show houses and walled gardens on the south side against the Passetto wall. The other side of the street has fewer houses and bigger gardens. The grand new basilica of Saint Peter's which was begun in 1506 is underway, though Bernini's triumphant colonnade will not be built for eighty years. The drum of Michelangelo's dome is complete. Saint Peter's Piazza has been enlarged by the demolition of the "island" of Saint Gregorio in Cortina. We see the diagonal lane— the Via di Pelegrini—coming in from the north toward the high Vatican wall and making for the newly constructed Porta Angelica gate. This is the route followed by pilgrims reaching Rome on the ancient Via Cassia. From Monte Mario, a mile away, travelers would have their first view of the eternal city.

Four years later in 1593, Antonio Tempesta's elegant woodcut plan of Rome was published. He created an extraordinary work of art out of a simple map, keeping its integrity while eddying and swirling the river and allowing the Hospital of

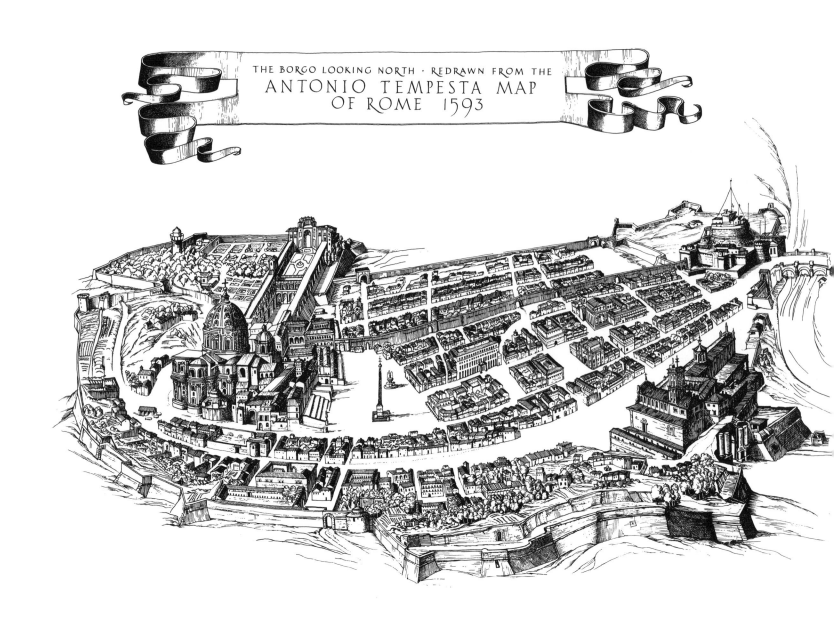

THE BORGO LOOKING NORTH · REDRAWN FROM THE
ANTONIO TEMPESTA MAP
OF ROME 1593

Santo Spirito to crest vigorously on its hill, almost stealing pride of place from Saint Peter's. The area of the borgo is shown as an approximate oval positioned just under the decorative ribbon that carries the inscription and Tempesta's name. The borgo's placement "across the river" is clear.

In detail we see the Via di Borgo Pio now completely lined with buildings on both sides. Its surroundings are very interesting. Via di Porta Angelica, which was a lane before the new fortified wall went in, now has an important gate and is the main entrance to the borgo from the north, bypassing the Via di Pelegrini. Nero's obelisk has been erected in Saint Peter's Piazza. The grand fountain in the piazza was installed by Bramante on orders of Alexander VI, who also had the gate of Saint Peter's rebuilt.

The Tempesta plan shows the Hospital of Santo Spirito as it was rebuilt in 1474 with Sixtus IV's elegant wing stretching from the river to the medieval gate of Santo Spirito. The so-called Octogon was also built then. The building today is the restoration of the hospital after its destruction by Charles V. The Octogon can be visited, and the hospital is still functioning. The enormously long halls once lined with beds have been subdivided and partitioned into recovery wards not open to the public.

When the Via di Borgo Pio opened, the modest architecture of the Middle Ages had already given way to the Renaissance. Bramante's Greek cross design for the new Saint Peter's was "to raise the Pantheon on the Basilica of Constantine"; a Renaissance concept that in the end was not carried out. A list of the architects that participated throughout the hundred-odd years of Saint Peter's gestation reads like a Hall of Fame: Bramante, Raphael, Sangallo, Peruzzi, Michelangelo, Vignola, Ligorio, Fontana, Maderno, and finally Bernini.

By 1562, the year the Via di Borgo Pio opened and thirty-five years after the terrible devastation wrought by Charles V's army, the borgo would have been almost completely rebuilt. The large blocks of buildings that show so clearly in the Tempesta map follow a simple pattern that in many respects was the same as the buildings of the Caesars—tenements several stories tall

surrounding an interior courtyard. Shops and workplaces were on the ground floor, and stairways led to living quarters above. The Via di Borgo Pio retains this pattern. In only one place has the palazzo form with no *bottega* on the ground floor replaced the shops.

In ancient Rome the shop on the ground floor was both the workplace and the store. We can see examples in Pompeii and Ostia. The door was a large opening with a counter closing it halfway, leaving the rest open for passage. Articles were made inside and sold over the counter to buyers outside. Christian Elling recalls seeing one or two relics of this style in Rome as late as the 1920s. Trajan's Markets, built in the early second century, have shop doors with handsome frames of travertine or marble that in a style has never left the scene. There are many like them on the Via di Borgo Pio.

Shop fronts habitually alternate with doorways that either lead immediately up the stairway to living quarters or proceed down the hall to the stairway. Elling analyzes this as a "rational line of houses, where each unit was composed of only one shop plus one front door leading to the inside stairs and the upper stories." The doorway/shop/doorway/shop was the vernacular architecture of Rome and has been copiously preserved. A double form of house was also very popular, wherein the outer doors or shops were moved as far to the sides of the building as possible, and the two inner ones were kept close together. Until the face lifts of this century, the horizontal divisions of the street façades were echoed vertically by the window divisions. Elling calls it a general rule that "the older the façade, the further the two windows have been moved to the sides, emphasizing the entity of the walls."

Doorways followed the style of the period in which they were built or renovated. The seventeenth century refined the portals, keeping the narrow doors and framing them with fluted pilasters of peperino or travertine and turning the ancient square window above into a semicircular light, open but protected with a grill. Variations on this theme are legion, exploiting the baroque features of broken pediments and volutes and the more lighthearted arabesques of the Rococo.

The Via di Borgo Pio was never the high class-street that the Via di Borgo Nuovo or the Via di Borgo Vecchio on the other side of the wall was. Elling has described this contrast in his inimitable

fashion: "and do not forget the gateways in the fortified corridor [Passetto] from Castel Sant' Angelo to the Vatican—the reek of people and smoke oozed out through them from Via di Borgo Pio's sidewalks into the prelate's highway." The Via di Borgo Pio was instead home to the low-level clergy, the bureaucrats of the Vatican, and the artisans that scratched away in the dark little shops that were everywhere on the north side of the Passetto. The Via degli Ombrellari, which crosses the Via di Borgo Pio, was where umbrellas were made. Something in their production caused a horrible smell, commented on by various sixteenth-century writers.

When the street first opened in 1562, there would have been several separate buildings to a block, with the leftover vacant spaces retaining their function as gardens surrounded by walls for security. As the rapid expansion of the area took place, the blocks filled with buildings and the gardens were relegated farther outside the walls to the Prati, which continued to be the provisioning fields for Rome.

The borgo came into its own, officially, in 1586 when it was designated as Rione XIV, one of the municipal divisions or districts of Rome. It had been a part of Rione XIII—Trastevere—but clearly it was a self-contained unit having little in common with the suburb down the river. Its free-standing status befitted the energy and coercive power of the new pope, Sixtus V, a man of action. The new Saint Peter's was much on his mind. He leaned so hard on his architects Giacomo della Porta and Domenica Fontana that the great dome designed by Michelangelo was completed in the brief span of only twenty months.

It was Sixtus who had the Egyptian obelisk that had been the focal point of Nero's circus moved to its present position in the piazza in front of the basilica. It weighed 350 tons and was 25.50 meters high, and it had to be moved 260 meters. The Renaissance workmen apparently did not have the experience nor the slave power that the ancients had when it came to moving around a ponderous and unwieldy work of art. Sixtus put the navy on the project, which, according to one source, commandeered forty-four winches, 140 horses, and nine hundred men. Another source claimed only 75 horses and eight hundred men. It is a familiar tale about how the crowd was cautioned on pain of death not to make a sound, but just as it looked as if the ropes would break

because they were chafing against the granite, a sailor shouted to wet the ropes, which solved the problem and saved the day.

Sixtus planned on a large scale. Part of the reason for moving the obelisk was his desire to change the Greek cross plan of the new basilica into a more spacious Latin cross. Enhancing the piazza by adding the Egyptian treasure would make a fitting termination to the longer nave.

Sixtus also had dark thoughts about demolishing the island or the *spina* of buildings that ran in front of the church down to the river. This would serve to open up a grand vista of the façade of Saint Peter's to arrivals coming from across the river. Money, or the lack of it, and Sixtus's death kept these two plans from being implemented in the sixteenth century.

Twenty years later, Paul V picked up Sixtus's project for radical change in the plan of the church. He put the architect Maderno in charge. It was Maderno's job to push the piazza even further to the east for a longer sight line, because extending the nave of the church would result in the new façade obscuring the view of the dome. To quote Elling again, "Maderno's façade was subjected to criticism in its time, but Michelangelo's dome and the mountain of a church beneath it were inviolable, possessing the eternal rights of perfection."

The design of an extended piazza, like the design of the church itself, provided through the years a fascinating collection of proposals from the luminaries of architecture.

Leon Battista Alberti drew up a bold geometric plan that called for a large rectangular area between Saint Peter's and the Castel Sant' Angelo, divided by three broad avenues with the obelisk in the center, and a huge extension of the square. He would have razed the *spina*.

The project of Carlo Fontana in 1694 showed his genius, but it would have entailed a wholesale rearrangement of the district. He wanted to demolish the *spina* as far as the Piazza Scossacavalli —about halfway to the river—and to continue Bernini's colonnade until that point.

During the reign of Pius VI, Cosima Morelli fiddled with Fontana's plan, increasing its grandiosity in a way that predictably appealed to Napoleon, but not to F. J. L. Meyer, who wrote a strong critique against the project in 1783. Meyer made clear the dichotomy that troubled aesthetes until the final solution was achieved—

or perpetrated, depending on your point of view. On one side was the desire for a grand and noble vista of Saint Peter's—a wide avenue to allow the faithful to experience from a distance the full scale of the mother church. On the other was the wish to retain the breathtaking shock that comes from the unexpected revelation of a masterpiece revealed after threading through the narrow streets and passing under the shadowy colonnade into an explosion of sun, space, fountains, and Maderno's majestic façade. The two points of view—an appreciation of grandeur versus the yearning for a moment of truth—can never coincide. In 1937 grandeur won. The *spina* was demolished, and the Via della Conciliazione opened up.

None of the early plans seemed to address one of the facts of life along the Tiber—namely its propensity for flooding. Regularly and destructively the waters rose, causing human misery and property damage. Only thirty-six years after the Via di Borgo Pio was opened, on Christmas night of 1598, a terrible flood swept away the parapets of the bridge and drowned the city. A marble plaque is mounted on the brick wall of the Hospital of Santo Spirito showing the water level.

This particular calamity did cause Urban VIII to reopen several arches of the bridge previously closed for aesthetic reasons, in order to allow the waters to pass more freely. Urban explained his reasons for this work on a plaque that also warned posterity not to repeat the same error. Instead, it was predictably repeated as soon as Gian Lorenzo Bernini created two huge buttresses to support his statues that decorated the bridge. Not until another great flood in 1870, when Rome was already the capital of Italy, was the decision made to wall the embankments.

In 1744 the most famous plan of Rome was published—that of Giovanni Batista Nolli. It was an ideal time for a new map, falling into that period of "urban lethargy" that followed the boiling creativity of the sixteenth- and seventeenth-century architects. It is once again, after an interval of 193 years, a modern map in plan form, not showing buildings as three dimensional. Nolli draws in detail the face of the borgo as it was remade in the style of the Renaissance and Baroque. We see clearly the outline of the basilica of Saint Peter as the apostle's key fitting into the keyhole shaped colonnade—a wonderful flight of baroque symbolism from the richly complex genius of Bernini.

Except for the urban restructuring that was part of the new Saint Peter's, the borgo escaped major change over and over through the centuries, while the rest of the city was buffeted by development. The Via di Borgo Pio particularly, with its back firmly planted against the Passetto and its heels dug in against encroachment from the north, kept its medieval self-containment throughout its 430-odd-year career. The Via di Borgo Vittorio, the next street to the north, is less homogenous, perhaps because the Via di Borgo Pio was providing most of the services necessary to the area, allowing the nearby streets to evolve in other ways. The familiar pattern of doorway/shop/doorway/shop faded in the northern parts of the grid which were farther removed from the busy pedestrian traffic flowing from Saint Peter's to the Sant'Angelo bridge.

Architecturally, two periods have stamped the Via di Borgo Pio. One encompassed the architects and architecture of Pius IX, that is, up until 1870; and the other involved the architects and architecture of Rome as the capital of Italy—from 1871 on.

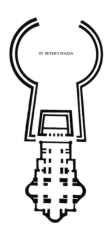

ST. PETER'S PIAZZA

Saint Peter's Basilica and Bernini's colonnade as key and keyhole.

The first period found Rome of the 1850s besieged with social ills. Efforts to provide more housing for the poor and other restructuring led to a profound change in the face of the *centro storico*. The change was less stringent in the Rione Borgo than in the rest of Rome. However, Pius IX did have a complex of nine houses built for the indigent on the narrow Via degli Ombrellari— presumably the nasty smelling umbrella works were a thing of the past—two schools for boys down at the piazza at the eastern end of the Via di Borgo Pio, and a large school for girls on the Via di Borgo Vittoria. Also constructed in 1870 was a granary or storage barn in the Via di Borgo Angelica. This last was not according to neighborhood standards and was later upgraded into a habitation. Four blocks away Pius restored the Hospital of Santo Spirito and added a hall for the mentally ill.

Continuing the good work, Pius IX refaced many buildings and sometimes added an additional story. This process was carried out in many other parts of Rome, causing a certain conformity to weave itself into the worn fabric of the city. The style chosen was that of the nobility and the bourgeoisie of the eighteenth century.

Gianfranco Spagnesi made a study of buildings in Rome that had lawful changes made in their façades from 1848 to 1905. When a building permit was applied for, a diagram was made of the existing façade and sometimes a diagram of what it was to look like after the renovation. The study shows that on the Via di Borgo Pio there were eleven building "interventions" between 1853 and 1872 and one in 1904. Nine asked for the addition of one new floor, three added two new floors, seven modernized the façade, two restructured the insides, and two joined two previously separate buildings.

The second period of definitive architecture was born of the unification of Italy, the naming of Rome as the capital, and the separation of powers between the state and the papacy. The psychological effect of the latter is evident. No longer ruling Rome and titularly all of Italy, the Vatican and its borgo today seem to float tranquilly on a sea of tourists and faithful, causing few ripples outside of its sheltered harbor.

In the 1890s the intact perimeter of the borgo was breached by the removal of Pius IV's fortified wall and the carving out of the Piazza del Risorgimento, allowing the grid of streets in the northern part of the borgo to bleed into the larger space of the new suburb of the Prati. The busy artery of Via di Porta Angelica received its smooth wall isolating it from the Vatican. The rest of the perimeter wall to the east, south, and west remains a visual and physical containment as it has for centuries.

Naturally the borgo was only part of the bigger picture. Changes there were nothing in comparison to what was happening on the other side of the river in the *centro storico*. The erection of the enormous Vittorio Emmanuela monument destroyed the scale and the ambiance of the Piazza Venezia, not to mention the irreplaceable loss of the ancient Roman houses on the Capitoline Hill.

The *systemazione* of the banks of the Tiber concurrent with the building of the Vittorio Emmanuela Bridge affected borgo and *centro* alike. The bridge was an attempt to open an easy way through the borgo to the burgeoning suburb of the Prati. It was the first new entry into the borgo from the city since the second century. The final implementation of this plan hung fire until 1937 when the state accomplished what had been too expensive and onerous for a long succession of popes. It was the destruction of the *spina* and the opening of the Via della Conciliazione. The agoniz-

ing amputations, immolations, and reconstructive surgery provoked by the project burned the toes of the Via di Borgo Pio. The entire first block of buildings on the east side of Via di Porta Angelica extending to the boundary of the borgo were razed in the 1940s and replaced by monolithic blocks in the style of Mussolini Modern.

As a result the first block of the Via di Borgo Pio was victimized—not in the eyes of all the inhabitants, however. One of the shop managers in that sterile and cheerless block confided to me that she thought the old part of the street was *brutta* (ugly). At least the direct leap that took Rome from the style of the eighteenth century to modern architecture spared the city the puffery of Victorian excesses. Chances are good that any further mutilations of the area have been stopped by the strict laws now governing development in the city.

The saga of Via della Conciliazione began with the demolition of the *spina*, that triangle of houses between the Via di Borgo Vecchio and the Via di Borgo Nuovo. The architects Spaccarelli and Piacentini supervised the destruction, in the course of which they discovered vestigial remains of the ancient pyramid. Preserved by being incorporated into the defensive walls of the fifteenth century, it had been partially demolished in 1499 by Alexander VI, but disappeared forever under Julius II.

In all, twenty-two buildings were torn down for the new development, plus dozens of small habitations that lined the walls of the Passetto in the north of the borgo and clung to the Hospital of Santo Spirito in the south. Of the three ancient roads that led from the bridge toward Saint

Peter's—Via di Borgo Santo Spirito, Via di Borgo Vecchio, Via di Borgo Nuovo—only Via di Borgo Santo Spirito remains. A new piazza, Piazza Pia, was formed at the Castel and joined to the new Piazza Giovanni XXIII. The two buildings that flank the beginning of Via della Conciliazione at the river were built in 1940 and the rusting wall fountains installed on their backsides in 1957. The venerable Church of San Michele Arcangelo was to fall, and the cannonball wall fountain that adjoined it was moved to its present position at the end of Via di Borgo Pio. Only two buildings on the

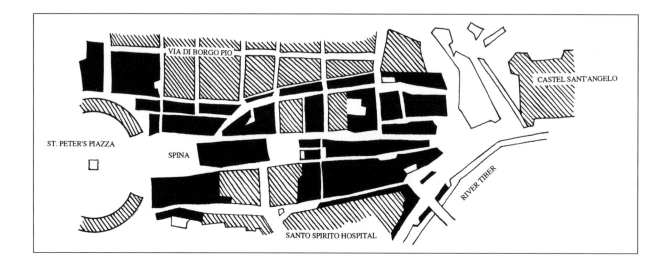

Map showing the borgo before the destruction of the spina. *Striped areas are untouched properties. Black denotes buildings demolished.*

Cannonball fountain at the end of the Via di Borgo Pio.

north side of Via della Conciliazione (Santa Maria in Traspontina and the white limestone block of the Palazzo Torlonia) and two buildings on the south side (the austere Palazzo dei Penitenzieri and the Palazzo Serristori) are original and in their original locations.

Today as we proceed along the Via della Conciliazione toward Saint Peter's, we have on the right the Church of Santa Maria in Traspontina. It had its origins near the Castello but was moved to this spot in 1564. Attached to its flank like a lavish doghouse is the tiny Oratorio della Dottrine

Cristiana, carried out in 1715 by Matteo Sassi. Inside there is a froth of exquisite rococo work in stucco and polychrome marble.

Next is another 1940s building. Following that we come to the other untouched mansion on the right side of Via della Conciliazione, the Palazzo Torlonia. It has similarities to the bigger Cancelleria across the river, which was built fifteen years earlier in 1485 and which some attribute to Bramante. Torlonia, though not a clone, is classic Renaissance, relying on scale and the harmonious relationship of the fenestration for its proud

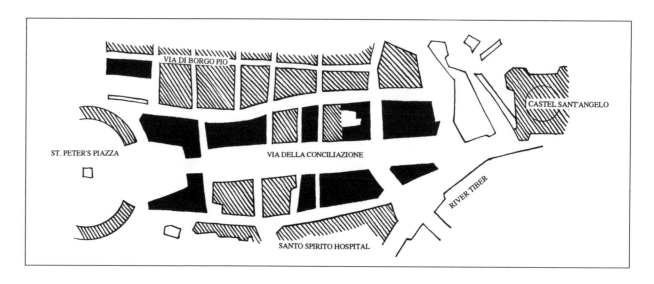

Map showing the borgo after construction of the Via della Conciliazione. Black areas are new buildings. Striped areas are original properties.

dignity, a relief from the constant presence of the highly charged Baroque.

Next to Torlonia is a building called the Convertendi, which originally occupied a spot in the *spina*, but was demolished in 1937 and reconstructed on this site.

The last of the old buildings is the Palazzo Bresciano, like the Convertendi torn down with the removal of the *spina* and rebuilt in this spot. The final colorless buildings with their square columned arcades just before the Bernini Colonnade are from 1940s and are called Propilei.

Turning and starting down the south side of Via della Conciliazione headed for the river is first the Palazzo Cesi, constructed in 1480 and completely rebuilt in 1577 by Martino Longhi. It has been transformed and reduced, though retaining a little of its noble sixteenth-century aura in the first floor *bugnati*, the portal with its Doric pilasters and the big lion's head on the corner. Connected to the Cesi is the enormous Palazzo dei Penitenzieri, which, in spite of its cruel introspective demeanor, is not a penitentiary, but derives its name from an order of Penitents. Built in 1480, it has the medieval air of the Palazzo Venezia,

although not relieved by Walt Disney crenelations along the roof line.

The last large complex before the modern building at the river is the Palazzo Alicorni, originally located where the southern Propilei is now.

Retracing one's steps back to the Propilei and rounding the corner of Via Rusticucci to cross the Via dei Corridori at the arches of the Via del Mascherino allows a clear view of the remaining wounds inflicted by the urban development plan of the Mussolini regime. The space hollowed out adjacent to the Bernini Colonnade where the Passetto reaches the Vatican is now the *capolinea* (bus terminus) of the never-ending stream of #64 buses. To the west of Via del Mascherino are the bald travertine and brick blocks that reach all the way to the Piazza del Risorgimento.

Notwithstanding these intrusions, the Via di Borgo Pio opens on the east, little changed in its urban character through the centuries. The street began with buildings of two or three floors in height, with shops on the ground floor, many receiving periodic refreshment of face and once in a while the addition of another story.

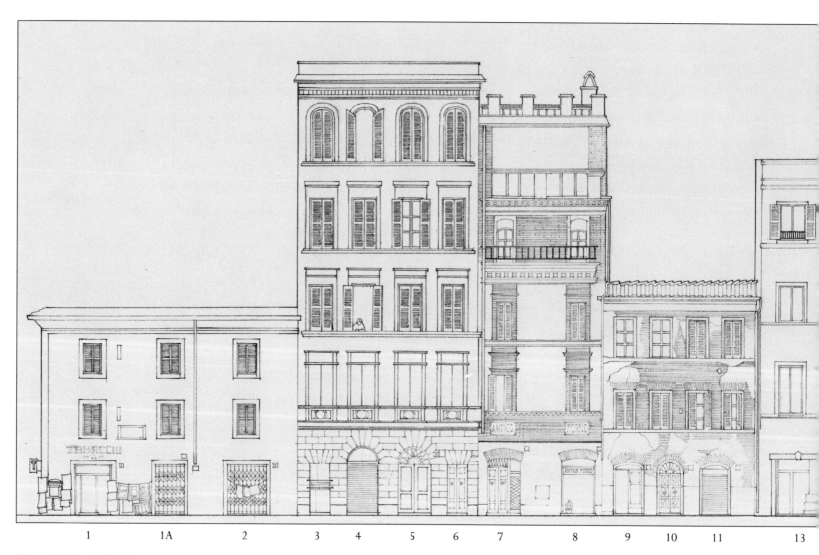

1   1A   2   3   4   5   6   7   8   9   10   11   13

VIA DI PORTA CASTELLO

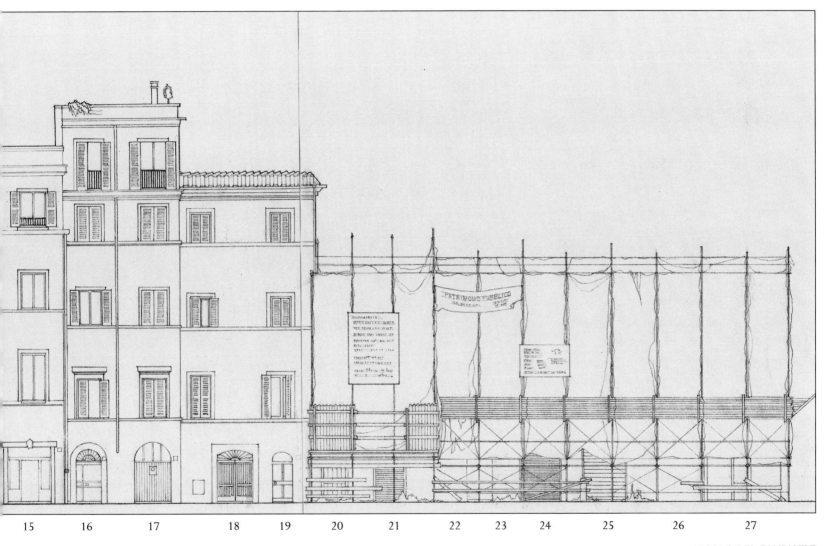

15 16 17 18 19 20 21 22 23 24 25 26 27

VICOLO DEL CAMPANILE

South Side of Via di Borgo Pio, Second Block

27A   28   29   29A   30   31   32   33   34

VICOLO DEL CAMPANILE

36   37   38   39   40   41   42   43   44   44A   45

VICOLO D' ORFEO

South Side of Via di Borgo Pio, Third Block

46   47   48   49   50   51

VICOLO D' ORFEO

53 54 55   56 57 58 59

VICOLO DELLE PALLINE

60   62   63   64   65   66   67   68

VICOLO DEL PALLINE

9 70 71 72 73 74 75 76 77

VICOLO DEL FARINONE

South Side of Via di Borgo Pio, Fifth Block

78   79   80   81   82   83   8

VICOLO DEL FARINONE

86   87   88   89   90   91   92   92A

VIA DEL MASCHERINO

41

South Side of Via di Borgo Pio,
Sixth Block

93   94   95

VIA DEL MASCHERINO

98   99   100   101

VIA DI PORTA ANGELICA

102

103

VIA DI PORTA ANGELICA

105   106   107

VIA DEL MASCHERINO

North Side of Via di Borgo Pio, Fifth Block

121   122   123   124   125   126   127

VIA DEL MASCHERINO

130   131   132   133   134   135

VIA DEL FALCO

North Side of Via di Borgo Pio, Fourth Block

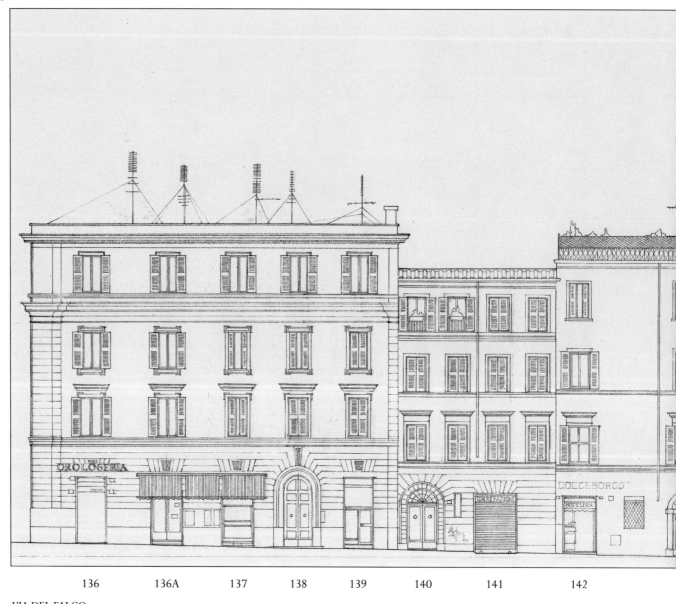

136   136A   137   138   139   140   141   142

VIA DEL FALCO

145   146   147   148   149   150   151   152

VIA PLAUTO

North Side of Via di Borgo Pio, Third Block

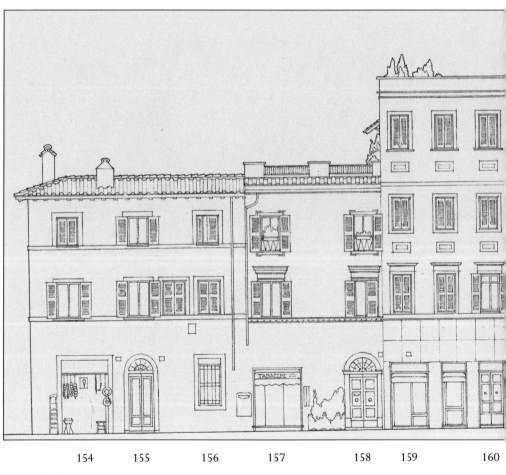

154   155   156   157   158   159   160

VIA PLAUTO

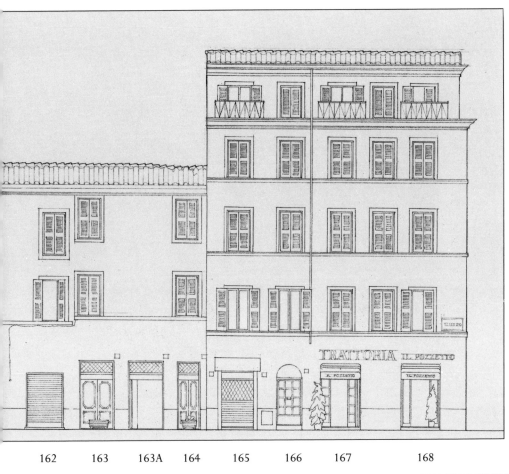

162   163   163A   164   165   166   167   168

VIA DEGLI OMBRELLARI

51

North Side of Via di Borgo Pio, Second Block

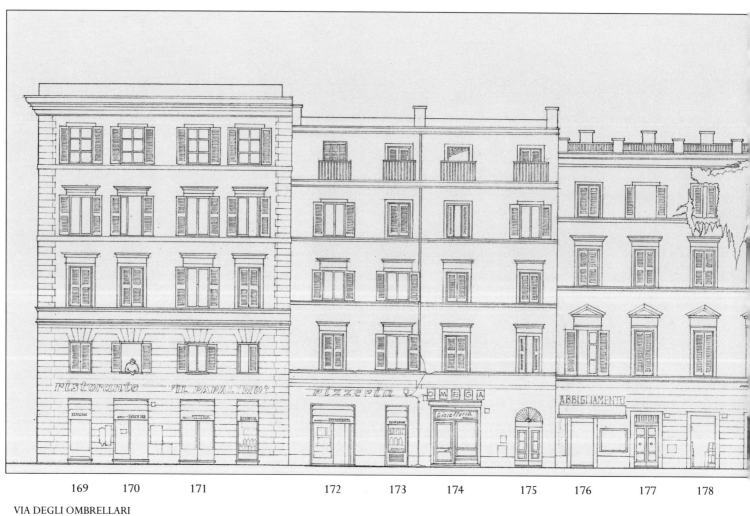

169   170   171   172   173   174   175   176   177   178

VIA DEGLI OMBRELLARI

179

180 181 181A 182 183

VIA DEI TRE PUPAZZI

53

North Side of Via di Borgo Pio, First Block

184 185 186 187 188 189 190 191 192 193 194 195

VIA DEI TRE PUPAZZI

196   202   203   204   205   206

VIA DI PORTA CASTELLO

"Backs" of the buildings of the Via di Borgo Pio against the Passetto.

The area of the borgo having the Via di Borgo Pio as its central axis remains today as it always has been, a quarter of workers, artisans, and petit bourgeoisie. The cross streets are pockmarked with furniture refinishers and small auto repair shops. In the dark cavelike alley between the Passetto wall and the "backs" of the buildings of the Via di Borgo Pio are sandwiched stone carvers' shops whose amazing supplies of marble are laid up in slabs like so much wallboard. Automobile body work is managed in the constricted space by a judicious juggling of cars into and out of pocket-sized shops. There are no signs of a hydraulic lift.

At the meeting of Vicolo del Farinone and the Passetto is a foundry where Francesco Lucenti makes bells of all types, petite to ponderous, some standing four feet tall. This little factory has been on this spot since 1550.

At numbers 131 through 134 Via di Borgo Pio, the building that is now the Hotel Santa Anna was constructed almost as soon as the street was opened in the 1560s. Its modest demeanor reveals its age, as do its three stories with outside windows pushed to the far edges and inner ones pressed together. The doors and windows of the ground floor have been modified through the centuries, but the fluted marble frames may well be original. At number 79 is a recently cleaned brick building dating from the 1700s which still has its original and popular rusticated portal.

Two other buildings on the Via di Borgo Pio are dated securely from the 1500s. Number 154/155 is proudly owned by the ironmonger who works out of his ground-floor shop. His charming tile-roofed house is marred only by a window which was added to the second floor, destroying the symmetry. Number 183 is in a parlous state, exposing its four-hundred-year-old wrinkles. The stucco skin that we see crumbling away is, of course, not original, but we can see the masonry skeleton, its poor bones being calcified by serious water leakage problems. Reconstructive work is going on, and in due course perhaps the building will be good for four hundred more years.

Between numbers 179 and 180, there is a tiny piazza that shelters a *fontanella* from which purls the water of the Acqua Marcia, cold, clear, and delicious. The fountain is a vertical rectangle of laid-up stone protected by a neat pediment. It carries the arms of the Camera Apostolica carved

Fontanella on the Via di Borgo Pio.

*Building in Borrominiesque style on the corner of the
Via di Borgo Pio and the Via del Falco.*

above the marble basin. There are almost always
people congregated at this spot, filling water jugs,
washing hands or fruit. When the Via di Borgo Pio
was created, the *piazzetta* was framed by the
houses of Giacomo Catalone, a rich Milanese
artisan who gave his name to the small square.

The Vicolo delle Palline has number 24,
constructed in the late 1500s, which was the home
of the architect Domenico Fontana in 1580. Also
on the Vicolo delle Palline, number 4/5 was built
in the early years of 1600 and retains its original
rusticated doorway. At number 11 is yet another
1600s building, restored in 1988, and at number
21/22 is a beautiful doorway of the 1600s.
Somewhere along here Ugo Valeri, resident architect for Saint Peter's and Bernini's so-called last
disciple, lived and died in 1786.

The one truly outstanding building is number
135 on the Via di Borgo Pio at the corner of Via
del Falco and is dated 1720. It is in serious
disrepair. Labeled by some as being
Borrominiesque because of its sculptural qualities,
it has rococo flourishes and whimsies. The
windows of the fourth floor are surmounted by
broken pediments enclosing scrolled frames with
deep recesses. The second-floor fenestration alter-

nates arched frames with pedimented ones, elaborated by a curled leaf motif. Grand pilasters form the corner of the building, blossoming into volutes supporting a section of curving architrave visually held in place by a large stucco star. The main entrance on the Via del Falco can only be described as wildly imaginative. The artist was Giuseppe Sardi, who was also responsible for the façade of the church of the Maddalena near the Pantheon. Sadly the Via di Borgo Pio building is deteriorating rapidly and the unique stucco decorations are flaking off. Residents of the street say that it is used as a cheap rooming house, and the owners have no money to restore it.

The Via di Borgo Pio is decorated in other, not so flamboyant ways. At the corner of the Vicolo del Campanile, at the second-floor level, is an eighteenth-century *edicola*, an image of Mary in a baroque stucco frame. Underneath is a plaque which promises two hundred days of plenary indulgence to all the faithful of either sex who stop to recite the litany under the sacred shrine—this, by decree of Pius VI in 1797. A few feet below the shrine and on the Via di Borgo Pio side of the corner is a very old "bread measure."

Window detail of Borrominiesque building.

Pilaster capital on Borrominiesque building.

The guide books say it was used to measure the size of loaves so that they would not be too small, thus cheating the poor. An old lady who engaged me in conversation assured me that, on the contrary, the pope decreed that bread could be no larger than the hole, so that he wouldn't lose in taxes.

At 70/71 Via di Borgo Pio is another *edicola*, this one newer and outlined (inside the carved stucco frame) with light bulbs and protected by glass. Vicolo delle Palline 19/20 has yet another, a Raphael Madonna illuminated by one bare bulb supported by two fat angels. It is protected from rain by a *baldachino* edged in metal scallops. One of the most interesting wall shrines is hidden under the arch of the Passetto at Vicolo d' Orfeo. It has a heavy wooden frame flanked with fluted Corinthian columns and a pediment that is a favorite perch for pigeons.

Not to be missed on the Vicolo del Campanile, which runs along the side of Santa Maria in Traspontina, is a Renaissance house with historiated wall paintings. It was a popular style of decoration at the end of the fifteenth century. These, although they have faded to a shadow, are the only remaining wall paintings in the borgo.

Sprinkled along the borgo's building façades are small metal plates carrying the name of various fire insurance companies and other plaques carved in stone that have to do with ownership of property. These, combined with residual signs of repair work, plumbing pipes, electric wires, television antenna connections, graffiti, and crumbling stone, make of the street a delightful pastiche enriched by the warm oranges, ochers, siennas, and reds of the stucco walls.

It is the activity on the street level with its noisy bustle and active social intercourse that has defined the personality of the Via di Borgo Pio from its inception until today. Out of the small cubicles for selling wares, out of the artisan's studios, and out of the repair shops spill the Romans, now as ever eager to engage in animated discussion with neighbors. The mothers with babies have their own cliques, augmented by the grandmothers *(nonnas)* and their energetic young-sters. Sitting on a bench and listening surreptitiously to the chatter is to hear the changeless banalities of civilization—children, politics, sport.

Corner of the Via di Borgo Pio and Vicolo del Campanile with edicola.

Edicola *under the arch of the Passetto at the Vicolo d' Orfeo.*

The Via di Borgo Pio is changing rapidly now. Gentrification, that wonderful word meaning that the haves are buying out the have-nots, is already evident in the blocks closest to the Vatican where well-to-do entrepreneurs are acquiring the shops that once provided the necessities of life and opening candle stores and yet other souvenir centers. More insidious is the transfer of real estate from the families that have lived in the borgo for generations to unknown landlords able to buy apartments or whole buildings at prices that locals can't turn down, and renovate them for sale or rent, frequently to foreigners or companies that want to keep an apartment in the heart of Rome. The Vatican owns much of the real estate in the area, but what effect, if any, this has on the social milieu is unknown.

In Rome, the time line is staggering. The ancient ruins, at a two-thousand-year remove, are difficult to recreate in the mind's eye. Baroque Rome is more accessible to the imagination than ancient Rome because there is more of it, but the speeded-up sightseeing favored nowadays hinders

rather than helps understanding. The tour bus dis-
gorging its single-flavored package of viewers in
front of sight after sight, picking them up, putting
them down, effectively obliterates any background
that could unify the disparate images.

Nevertheless, we have the medium of a mod-
est street, still alive, still functioning with its allu-
sions to the Baroque intact. It is a bridge that can
be flung across the centuries. A stroll along the
Via di Borgo Pio, preferably in the direction of
the Vatican, colors the canvas Roman, adds the
details of people, vegetables, sounds, crucifixes,
and the ineffable odor of coffee to the compo-
sition. Looking toward the ornate iron gates of
the Vatican is to glimpse the Seicento personified
in the dashing but serious young guards in black
capes and berets. To the left, shadowing the
Passetto is Bernini's quadruple colonnade, a
dark forest of columns through which the eager
pilgrim presses, stepping out into the vast, sun-
filled piazza, genius designed to simulate in
chiaroscuro the great C chord of "Let There Be
Light."

The urban renewal of 1938 wiped out this
ecstatic experience for the masses that approach

View of the Via di Borgo Pio today.

The Santa Anna Gates of the Vatican.

Saint Peter's from the river, who now look down the wide, exposed, honorific but dull Via della Conciliazione. The view does enhance the majesty of Michelangelo's dome—visible from this distance as it is not from the side streets—floating regally above its domain, its presence animating the borgo. From its beginning in 1506, the dome dominated the basilica as the Catholic Church dominated the people. Under its protection the Vatican consolidated; the *rione* blossomed; and the gardens, and later the buildings and shops, of the Via di Borgo Pio took up their positions. Today with the power of Catholicism stabilized and its dominance in the arena of the city severely curtailed by the Lateran Treaty of 1929, the dome, which was once an analog for the universe, now represents precisely 108 acres of the Vatican City. Appendages like the Passetto, the Via di Borgo Pio, the Via di Borgo Santo Spirito, even the Via della Conciliazione, no longer are nourished by an umbilical cord to the mother church, but prosper from a different source. The image we see as we walk along the Via di Borgo Pio is like a hologram that originates from a certain reality but through which we can pass our hands and our foreign voices. It is the tourist class that supports every aspect of commerce in the borgo, while at the same time it changes what it seeks most to retain—the illusion of time past.

Inside the Santa Anna Gates looking down the Via di Borgo Pio.

Appendix

INVENTORY OF GROUND FLOOR OCCUPANCY ON THE BORGO PIO, SPRING 1992

Every door is numbered, whether house or shop. Where modifications have been made—new doors punched or filled in—letters are used.

The designation "door" refers to an entry that will lead to the stairway to living quarters. The designation "shop" refers to direct access to a commercial establishment. (Names in quotation marks are actual names of shops.)

This inventory begins at the east end of Via di Borgo Pio at the Via di Porta Castello, runs down the south side to the Via di Porta Angelica where it turns back and comes down the north side, finishing at the Via di Porta Castello.

South Side of Via di Borgo Pio, East to West

Bld. 1	1	Shop. "Tabacchi" (tobacco shop)
	1 A	Shop. Permanently closed?
	2	Shop. Permanently closed?
Bld. 2	3	Window barred and shuttered closed.
	4	Shop. Permanently closed?
	5	Double doors. Permanently closed?
	6	Door.

Bld. 3   7   Door.

8   Shop. "Antico Forno" (bakery)

Bld. 4   9   Shop. Permanently closed?

10   Door.

11   Shop. Permanently closed?

Bld. 5   12   Number not visible.

13   Shop.

14   Door.

15   Shop.

Bld. 6   16   Door.

17   Shop.

Bld. 7   18   Number not visible. Shop.

19   Door.

Bld. 8   20   Door. This building has been under
restoration for twelve years.

21   Shop.

22   Once a door.

23   Shop.

24   Shop.

25   Door.

26   Door.

27   Shop.

*End of Block One. Vicolo del Campanile /
Via dei Tre Pupazzi*

Bld. 1   27A   Shop. "Pizza" (pizzeria)

28   Shop. *Alimentari* (grocery store)

Bld. 2   29   Door.

29A   Shop. "Macelleria" (butcher's shop)

30   Door.

31   Shop. Bar "Latteria" (dairy)

Bld. 3   32   Door.

33   Shop.

Bld. 4   34   Shop. "Quattrifolio" (lighting fixtures)

35   Door.

Bld. 5   36   Shop.

37   Door.

Bld. 6   38   Shop. "Pizzeria Da Peppino" (pizzeria)

39   Door.

Bld. 7   40   Shop. "Le Tre Maschere Gelateria
Artigiana" (ice cream shop)

41   Door.

Bld. 8   42   Shop.

43   Shop.

44   Door.

44A   Tiny door / window?

45   Shop. "Farmacia" (pharmacy)

End of Block Two. Vicolo d' Orfeo / Via degli Ombrellari

Bld 1   46   Shop.

47   Door.

48   Shop. "Latteria" (dairy, ice cream store)

Bld. 2   49   Door.

50   Shop.

Bld. 3 51 Door.

52 Shop. *Alimentari* (grocery store)

Bld. 4 53 Shop. "Luce" (lighting fixtures)

54 Door.

Bld. 5 55 Shop. "Frutteria" (fruit store)

56 Door.

Bld. 6 57 Door.

58 Shop. *Cose Diverse* (sundries)

59 Shop. *Alimentari* "Pane" (bread store)

End of Block Three. Vicolo delle Palline / Via Plauto

Bld. 1 60 Shop. *Ristorante* "Al Passetto di Borgo, da Roberto"

61 Shop. Part of above, not marked, no opening.

62 Shop. *Ristorante* "da Roberto" same as above.

63 Shop. "Borgo Shop" (gifts, souvenirs, Kodak film)

64 Door.

65 Shop. "Pulitura a Secco" (dry cleaning)

Bld. 2 66 Door.

No number. Shop. "Antica Salumeria" (delicatessen)

67 Shop. (same as above) "Formaggi" (cheese store)

Bld. 3 68 Door.

69 Shop.

Bld. 4 70 Door.

71 Shop. "Frutteria" (fruit store)

Bld. 5 72 Shop. "Tipographia Rilievografia" (printing and surveying)

73 Door.

Bld. 6 74 Shop. "Articoli Religiosi, Souvenir of Rome" (religious articles)

75 Shop. "Parrucchiere per Signora" (women's hairdresser)

76 Door.

77 Shop.

End of Block Four. Vicolo del Farinone / Via del Falco

Bld. 1 78 Shop. *Macelleria* (butcher shop)

79 Door.

80 Shop. "1000 Articoli, Giocattoli" (objets d'art and games)

Bld. 2 81 Door.

82 Shop. "Articoli Religiosi" "Factory" (religious articles)

Bld. 3 83 Shop. "Turella Adriana" (frame store and toys)

84 Door.

Bld. 4 85 Shop. "Interottica, ottica Lenti a Contacco" (glasses and contact lenses)

86 Shop? Was old door? "Ottica" (glasses)

Bld. 5 87 Shop. "Trattoria Marcello" (restaurant)

88 Door.

89 Shop window. (clerical outfitter)

90 Shop. "Mancinelli" (clerical outfitter)

Bld. 6 91 Door.

92 Shop. "Gran Mariani, Trattoria" (restaurant)

Bld. 7 92 (number repeated) Shop.

92A Shop. "Bar, Milk & Coffe"

End of Block Five. Via del Mascherino

Block Six is all one building.

93 Number not visible. Shop window. "Wama" (furniture store)

94 Shop. "Armadi" (not marked, window) (office furnishings)

95 Shop window. "Guarda Roba" (office furnishings)

96, 97 Numbers not visible. Driveway into apartments.

98 Shop. "Snack bar, Self Service, Tavola Calda"

99 Shop. "Self Service, Snack Bar, Pizzeria, Gelateria" (pizzeria and ice cream shop)

100 Shop. "Snack Bar, Self Service, Caffé S. Anna" (coffee shop)

101 Shop. "Rosaries, corals, glass, Murano"

End of Block Six. Via di Porta Angelica

North Side of Via di Borgo Pio, West to East

Block Six is all one building.

102 Window of shop. Articoli religiosi. (religious articles)

103 Garage entrance.

104 Volkswagen auto display.

105 Garage entrance.

106 Shop. "Agenzia Fotografica Vicenzo Modica" (photo store)

107 Shop. (entrance on Via del Mascherino) Window. *Articoli religiosi*. (religious articles)

End of Block Six. Via del Mascherino

Bld. 1 121 Shop. *Libreria* (no numbers between 107 and 121) (book store)

122 Shop. Same as above.

123 Door.

124 Shop. Closed permanently?

Bld. 2 125 Door.

126 Number not visible. Shop. *Alimentari*. (grocery store)

Bld. 3 127 Door to bar "Boncaffe Bondolfi" (coffee shop)

128 Shop. Same bar as above.

129 Shop. "Ricordi di Roma, Souvenir" (souvenirs of Rome)

130 Door.

Bld. 4 131 Shop. TV equipment.

132 Window of Santa Anna Hotel.

133 Door of Santa Anna Hotel.

134 Door (not used) of Santa Anna Hotel.

Bld. 5 135 Door. "Ristorante Artú a S. Pietro" (restaurant)

End of Block Five. Via del Falco / Vicolo del Farinone

Bld. 1 136 Shop. "Sara Watch, Orologeria"(watch shop)

136A Door to Snack Bar "Time Out"

137 Window of Snack Bar "Time Out"

138 Door.

139 Shop. Handmade leather goods.

Bld. 2 140 Door.

141 Shop. "Torrefazione"

Bld. 3 142 Shop. "Pasticceria" (pastry shop)

143 Door.

Bld. 4 144 Door.

145 Shop. T shirts, souvenirs.
No number. Shop. Same shop as above.

Bld. 5 146 Number not visible. Shop. "Bar Sergio"

147 Shop. "Rocchi Longines" (watches and jewelry)

148 Shop. "Polleria Macelleria" (meat and poultry)

149 Shop. "Curiosita, Bomboniere" (candy store)

150 Door.

151 Shop. "Comandini, Ingrosso, Articoli Religiosi" (wholesale religious articles)

152 Shop window. Same as above.

End of Block Four. Via Plauto / Vicolo delle Palline

Bld. 1 154 (There appears to be no number 153.)
Shop. "Ferramenta Pieroni" (hardware)

155 Door.

156 Number not visible. Window.

Bld. 2 157 Shop. "Tabacchi: Cartoleria Regali" (tobacco and postcard shop)

158 Door.

Bld. 3 159 Shop. "Al Vecchio Forno" (mostly bread)

160 Door.

Bld. 4 161 Door.

162 Shop. "Orient Express" (bar)

163 Window of Hotel della Conciliazione

163A Door of above.

164 Door.

Bld. 5 165 Shop. Closed permanently?

166 Door.

167 Shop. "Trattoria Il Pozzetto" (restaurant)

168 Door.

End of Block Three. Via degli Ombrellari / Vicolo d' Orfeo

Bld. 1 169 Number not visible. Window of Scialanga Snack Bar

170 Shop. "Scialanga Snack Bar"

171 Shop. "Il Papaline Ristorante: Birreria" (restaurant and beer store)

Bld. 2 172 Shop. Continuation of Scialanga restaurant.

173 Window of Scialanga restaurant.

174 Shop. "Gioielleria Segatori" (Omega watch shop)

175 Door.

Bld. 3 176 Shop. "Abbigliamento: Mercerie" (clothing store)

177 Door.

178 Shop. *Cose Diverse* (sundries)

178A Shop. Same as above.

Bld. 4 179 Shop. Fruit and vegetables.

Break in the block for a fountain.

Bld. 1 180 Shop. "Hostaria Il Mozzicone" (restaurant)

181 Door.

181A Shop. "Pescheria San Marinella" (fish market)

Bld. 2 182 Door.

183 Shop. "Hostaria dei 3 Pupazzi" (restaurant)

End of Block Two. Via dei Tre Pupazzi / Vicolo del Campanile

Bld. 1 184 Shop. Closed permanently?

185 Door.

186 Shop. "Snack Bar"

187 Shop. Same as above.

Bld. 2 188 Shop. "Quick Sec" (dry cleaning)

189 Shop. Same as above.

190 Shop. Closed permanently?

191 Door.

192 Shop. Closed permanently?

193 Shop. Closed permanently?

Bld. 3 194 Shop. "Armadi Guardaroba Assetta Letti in Ottone" (wardrobes and brass beds)

195 Door.

Bld. 4 196 Door. Big apartment block. No shops.

Bld. 5 202 (no numbers between 196 and 202) Shop. Closed permanently?

203 Door.

Bld. 6 204 Shop. Antiques.

205 Shop. Closed permanently?

206 Shop window. "Gelateria, Snack Bar" (ice cream, snacks)

End of Block One. Via di Porta Castello

Bibliography

Le Antiche Rovine di Roma nei Disegni di Du Perac. Ed. Silvana Editoriale. Roma: Amilcare Pizzi editore, 1990.

Arbeiter, Achim. *Alt St. Peter in Geschichte und Wissenschaft.* Berlin: Gebr. Mann Verlag, 1988.

Benevolo, Leonardo. *L'Architetture della citta nell'Italia contemporanea.* Bari: Editori Latenza, 1968.

Canezza, Alessandro. *Roma nei suoi rioni: XIV Borgo.* Roma: Fratelli Palombi editrici, 1936.

D'Onofrio, Cesare. *Castel S. Angelo e Borgo tra Roma e Papato.* Roma: Romana societa editrice, 1978.

Elling, Christian. *Rome: The Biography of Her Architecture from Bernini to Thorvaldson.* Boulder: Westview Press: 1936.

Francia, Ennio. *Storia della costruizione del nuovo S. Pietro.* Roma: De Luca editore, 1977.

Frutaz, Amato Patro. A cura di Amato Pietro Frutaz. *Le Piante di Roma.* 3 Vols. Roma: Istituo di studi romani. 1962.

Gadol, Joan. *Leon Battista Alberti: Universal Man of the Early Renaissance.* Chicago: University of Chicago Press, 1969.

Gigli, Laura. *Guide Rionali di Roma: Rione XIV Borgo.*

Parte Prima. Roma: Fratelli Palombi
Editori, 1990.

Gigli, Laura. *Guide Rionali di Roma: Rione XIV Borgo.*
Parte Seconda. Roma: Fratelli Palombi
Editori, 1992.

Krautheimer, Richard. *Rome: Profile of a City
312–1308.* Princeton: Princeton University
Press, 1980.

Kreig, Paul M. *San Pellegrino: Die Schweizerische
Nationalkirche in Rom.* Zurich: NZN
Buchverlag AG, 1974.

Lombardi, Perrucalo. *Roma: Palazzi, Palazzetti, Case.
Progetto per un inventario 1200–1870.* Roma:
Edilstampa, 1991.

Partner, Peter. *Renaissance Rome 1500–1559: A
Portrait of a Society.* Berkeley: University of
California Press, 1976.

Platner, Samuel Ball. *The Topography and Monuments
of Ancient Rome.* Boston: Allyn and Bacon,
1904.

Spagnesi, Gianfranco. *Edilizia Roman nella seconda
meta del XIX secolo.* Roma: Edizioni depco,
n.d.

Storoni, Paula Boccardi. *Storia della basilica di S.
Pietro.* Pavia: Editoriale Viscontea, 1888.

Tesei, Giovanni. *Storia, arte, e leggende del Rione
Borgo.* Roma: Anthropos, 1988.

Vannelli, Valter. *Economia dell'architetture in Roma
liberale.* Roma: Edizioni Kappa, 1981.

Vannelli, Valter. *Economia dell'architetture in Roma
fascista.* Roma: Edizioni Kappa, 1981.

Westfall, Carroll William. *In This Most Perfect
Paradise: Alberti, Nicholas V and the Invention of
Conscious Urban Planning in Rome, 1447–55.*
University Park, Pa.: Pennsylvania State
University Press, 1974.

de Wolfe, Ivor. *The Italian Townscape.* London: The
Architectural Press, 1963.

Zeppegno, Luciano. *Irioni di Roma.* Roma: Newton
Compton editori, 1978.